*Tailwind CSS unveiled:
work of an author hiding behind style sheets.*

Roberto Rescigno

Index

Tailwind CSS: a guide to using the popular utility-first CSS framework

Tailwind CSS is a CSS framework that allows you to quickly create responsive, well-designed user interfaces using predefined, composable CSS classes. In this guide, we will explore how to get started with Tailwind CSS and look at some development examples.

Introduction

Tailwind CSS is a modern and highly customizable CSS framework that is gaining increasing popularity among web developers. Comparing it with other popular frameworks such as Bootstrap, Foundation, and Bulma, we can point out some key differences that make Tailwind CSS an excellent choice for creating responsive user interfaces and design.

Bootstrap is one of the most popular and widely used CSS frameworks, known for its wide range of predefined components, responsive grid, and ease of use. However, Bootstrap has some limitations, such as the difficulty of customization, the presence of default styles that can make sites look similar to each other, and the use of semantically descriptive name-based classes, which can make the code less readable and difficult to maintain.

Tailwind CSS differs from Bootstrap and other similar frameworks in several ways:

1. **Utility-first** approach: Tailwind CSS follows a utility-first approach, which means it provides a set of atomic CSS classes that can be combined to create unique, custom user interfaces. This approach makes the code more readable, maintainable, and scalable, allowing developers to have more control over the style and structure of their Web site.

2. **Customization**: Tailwind CSS is extremely customizable, allowing developers to easily change colors, spacing, font sizes and other CSS properties directly in the configuration file. This makes it possible to create user interfaces that exactly reflect the desired design and branding, without having to wrestle with predefined styles or selectively override CSS rules.

3. **Lightness and performance**: Due to its modular nature and integration with optimization tools such as PurgeCSS, Tailwind CSS can produce much lighter final CSS files than other frameworks. This ensures faster page loading and a better user experience, especially on mobile devices and slow connections.

4. **Extensibility**: Tailwind CSS can be easily extended with custom plugins and components, allowing developers to add new features and utility classes as needed. This flexibility makes Tailwind CSS suitable for a wide range of projects and allows a tailored development toolkit to be created for each team.

5. **Integration with JavaScript frameworks**: Tailwind CSS can be integrated with popular JavaScript frameworks such as React, Vue, and Angular, allowing developers to use utility classes and custom components in conjunction with application logic and state.

Although Bootstrap and other CSS frameworks offer a quick and practical solution for creating responsive user interfaces, Tailwind CSS stands out for its flexibility, customization, light weight, and utility-first approach.

These features make Tailwind CSS an excellent choice for developers seeking greater control over the design and structure of their Web site without sacrificing ease of use and productivity.

While Bootstrap and other similar frameworks provide a set of ready-to-use predefined components, Tailwind CSS encourages developers to create their own components and layouts using utility classes.

This approach reduces dependence on predefined styles and components, allowing for the creation of more unique user interfaces in line with project requirements.

In addition, the Tailwind CSS community is constantly growing and offers resources, tutorials, and plugins that can help developers make the most of the framework's potential.

The official Tailwind CSS documentation is extremely comprehensive and up-to-date, providing a solid foundation for learning and using the framework.

Tailwind CSS's versatility makes it suitable for a wide range of projects, from static websites to dynamic and complex web applications. Whether you are a novice developer or a seasoned professional, Tailwind CSS offers a modern and flexible solution for creating responsive user interfaces and designs with ease and precision.

In summary, Tailwind CSS emerges as a leading framework in the landscape of user interface development tools because of its flexibility, light weight, and utility-first approach.

If you are looking for a framework that allows you to have complete control over the design of your website and create custom interfaces while maintaining excellent performance, Tailwind CSS is an ideal choice.

Here is a table highlighting the main differences between some of the most popular CSS frameworks, including Tailwind CSS, Bootstrap, Foundation and Bulma:

Features	Tailwind CSS	Bootstrap	Foundation	Bulma
Approach	Utility-first	Component-based	Component-based	Component-based
Customization	High	Moderate	Moderate	Moderate
Performance	High	Media	Media	Media
Responsive Grid	Yes	Yes	Yes	Yes
Predefined components	No (do it your self)	Yes	Yes	Yes
Modular	High	Media	Media	Media
JS Integration	Excellent	Good	Good	Good
Accessibility	Good	Good	Good	Good
Documentation	Excellent	Excellent	Good	Good
Community	Growing	Extended	Extended	Moderate

This table highlights some of the main differences between the various CSS frameworks in terms of approach, customization, lightweighting, default components, extensibility, integration with JavaScript frameworks, accessibility, documentation, and community.

It is important to note that choosing the most suitable framework depends on the specific requirements of your project and your personal preferences as a developer.

Installation (basic)

1. Installation of Tailwind CSS

To get started, you need to install Tailwind CSS in your project. If you are using a Node.js-based project, you can install Tailwind CSS via npm or yarn.

```
npm install tailwindcss
```

or

```
yarn add tailwindcss
```

After installing Tailwind CSS, you need to import it into your main stylesheet. Create a CSS file (e.g., styles.css) and add the following code:

```
@import 'tailwindcss/base';
@import 'tailwindcss/components';
@import 'tailwindcss/utilities';
```

Finally, include the CSS file in your HTML file:

```
<link href="/path/to/your/styles.css" rel="stylesheet">
```

2. Configuring Tailwind CSS

Tailwind CSS offers an optional configuration file that allows you to customize the design of your project. To create it, run the following command:

```
npx tailwindcss init
```

This command will generate a tailwind.config.js file in the root directory of your project. You can edit this file to customize colors, fonts, and other design settings.

```
module.exports = {
    purge: [],
    darkMode: false,
    theme: {
        extend: {
            backgroundColor: {
                'primary': '#1D4ED8',
                'secondary': '#9CA3AF',
            },
            fontFamily: {
                'sans': ['Roboto', 'Helvetica', 'Arial', 'sans-serif'],
            },
        },
    },
    variants: {
        extend: {},
    },
    plugins: [],
  }
}
```

3. Use of utility classes

Tailwind CSS uses a utility class approach to creating user interfaces. Utility classes are predefined CSS classes that can be combined to quickly create custom designs.

Here are some examples of utility classes:

bg-blue-500: Sets the background color to blue.

text-white: Sets the text color to white.

px-4: Adds a horizontal padding of 4 units.

rounded: Adds a rounded edge.

Here is an example of how to use utility classes to create a button:

```html
<button class="bg-blue-500 hover:bg-blue-700 text-white font-bold py-2 px-4 rounded">
    Button text
</button>
```

In this example, we used the following utility classes:

bg-blue-500: Sets the background color of the button to blue.

hover:bg-blue-700: Sets the background color of the button to dark blue when hovered over.

text-white: Sets the color of the button text to white.

font-bold: Sets the font style of the button text to bold.

py-2: Adds a vertical padding of 2 units to the button.

px-4: Adds a horizontal padding of 4 units to the button.

rounded: Adds a rounded border to the button.

4. Responsive components

Tailwind CSS makes it easy to create responsive designs using utility classes. To make a component responsive, simply add utility classes with prefixes for the desired breakpoints. The default breakpoints are sm, md, lg and xl.

Here is an example of how to use responsive utility classes to change the arrangement of an image and text based on the width of the device:

```html
<div class="flex flex-col sm:flex-row items-center">
  <img class="w-full sm:w-1/2" src="path/to/image.jpg" alt="Example">
  <div class="text-center sm:text-left mt-4 sm:mt-0 sm:ml-6">
    <h1 class="text-3xl">Title</h1>
    <p class="text-lg">Description</p>
  </div>
</div>
```

In this example, the main div uses flex flex-col sm:flex-row to create a columnar layout on mobile devices (flex flex-col) and a row layout on larger screens (sm:flex-row).

5. Examples of development with Tailwind CSS

<u>Example 1: Card</u>

Here is an example of a simple card made with Tailwind CSS:

```html
<div class="max-w-md mx-auto bg-white rounded-xl shadow-md overflow-hidden">
  <div class="md:flex">
    <div class="md:flex-shrink-0">
      <img class="h-48 w-full object-cover" src="path/to/image.jpg" alt="Example">
    </div>
    <div class="p-8">
      <h2 class="text-xl font-semibold">Card title</h2>
      <p class="mt-2 text-gray-500">Short description of the card.</p>
    </div>
  </div>
</div>
```

<u>Example 2: Navbar</u>

Here is an example of a simple navbar made with Tailwind CSS:

```html
<header class="bg-blue-500 text-white shadow">
  <nav class="container mx-auto flex items-center justify-between p-4">
    <div class="text-xl font-semibold">
      Site name
    </div>
    <ul class="hidden sm:flex space-x-4">
      <li><a href="#" class="hover:text-blue-300">Home</a></li>
      <li><a href="#" class="hover:text-blue-300">Products</a></li>
      <li><a href="#" class="hover:text-blue-300">Contacts</a></li>
    </ul>
    <button class="sm:hidden">
      <svg class="w-6 h-6" fill="none" viewBox="0 0 24 24"
stroke="currentColor">
        <path stroke-linecap="round" stroke-linejoin="round" stroke-
width="2" d="M4 6h16M4 12h16M4 18h16" />
      </svg>
    </button>
  </nav>
</header>
```

In this example, we created a navbar with a logo and a list of links.

The link list is hidden on mobile devices (hidden sm:flex) and is displayed only on larger screens.

We also added a menu icon for mobile devices, which is displayed only on smaller screens (sm:hidden).

<u>Example 3: Product grid</u>

Here is an example of a product grid made with Tailwind CSS:

```html
<div class="grid grid-cols-1 sm:grid-cols-2 md:grid-cols-3 gap-4">
  <div class="bg-white rounded-lg shadow-md p-4">
    <img class="w-full h-48 object-cover mb-4" src="path/to/image1.jpg" alt="Product 1">
    <h3 class="text-lg font-semibold">Product 1</h3>
    <p class="text-gray-500">Product Description 1</p>
  </div>
  <div class="bg-white rounded-lg shadow-md p-4">
    <img class="w-full h-48 object-cover mb-4" src="path/to/image2.jpg" alt="Product 2">
    <h3 class="text-lg font-semibold">Product 2</h3>
    <p class="text-gray-500">Product Description 2</p>
  </div>
  <div class="bg-white rounded-lg shadow-md p-4">
    <img class="w-full h-48 object-cover mb-4" src="path/to/image3.jpg" alt="Product 3">
    <h3 class="text-lg font-semibold">Product 3</h3>
    <p class="text-gray-500">Product description 3</p>
  </div>
</div>
```

In this example, we used the grid class and its derivatives to create a responsive grid of products that automatically adjusts the number of columns based on the width of the screen.

In conclusion, Tailwind CSS is a powerful and flexible framework that allows you to quickly create responsive and well-designed user interfaces using predefined and composable utility classes.

By following this basic guide, you should be able to start using Tailwind CSS for your web projects.

Installation (advanced)

Installing Tailwind CSS is a critical step to begin using the framework in your project. In this section, we will delve into the installation of Tailwind CSS, taking into account the different development environments and possible build tools.

Installation via CDN

If you want to get started quickly without setting up a Node.js-based development environment, you can use a CDN (Content Delivery Network) to include Tailwind CSS in your project. Add the following link in your HTML file, inside the `<head>` tag:

```html
<link href="https://cdn.jsdelivr.net/npm/tailwindcss@2.2.16/dist/tailwind.min.css" rel="stylesheet">
```

However, keep in mind that using a CDN does not allow you to customize Tailwind CSS configuration and may not be the ideal option for larger or more complex projects.

Installation via Node.js

For Node.js-based projects, installing Tailwind CSS via npm or yarn is the recommended approach. This way, you can take advantage of all the features and customizations offered by the framework.

1. Installing Tailwind CSS as a dependency

Open the terminal in the root directory of your project and install Tailwind CSS as a dependency, using one of the following commands:

With npm:

```
npm install tailwindcss
```

With yarn:

```
yarn add tailwindcss
```

2. Creating the main style sheet

After installing Tailwind CSS, you need to import it into your main stylesheet. Create a CSS file (e.g. `styles.css`) in the root directory of your project and add the following code:

```
@import 'tailwindcss/base';
@import 'tailwindcss/components';
@import 'tailwindcss/utilities';
```

3. Compilation of style sheet

At this point, you need to configure your build tool to process the main stylesheet and generate the final CSS file.

You can use different tools, such as PostCSS, Webpack, Gulp or others, depending on your preferences and development environment.

For example, if you are using PostCSS, create a `postcss.config.js` configuration file in the root directory of your project and add the following code:

```
module.exports = {
  plugins: {
    tailwindcss: {},
    autoprefixer: {},
  },
}
```

Next, run the following command to compile your style sheet:

```
npx postcss styles.css -o output.css
```

Where `styles.css` is your main stylesheet and `output.css` is the compiled CSS file that will be generated.

4. Include the completed style sheet

Finally, include the compiled CSS file in your HTML file:

```
<link href="/path/to/your/output.css" rel="stylesheet">
```

Where /path/to/your/output.css is the path to the compiled CSS file generated in step 3. By including this link in your HTML file, you will have access to all the utility classes and components of Tailwind CSS to create your design.

In summary, installing Tailwind CSS can be done in several ways depending on your needs and development environment.

Using a CDN is a quick option for simpler projects, but to take full advantage of the features and customizations offered by the framework, it is recommended to install Tailwind CSS via npm or yarn in a Node.js-based development environment.

Remember to properly configure your build tool and include the compiled stylesheet in your HTML file.

Configuration of Tailwind CSS (advanced)

One of the most appreciated features of Tailwind CSS is its highly customizable configuration. You can control all aspects of the design, such as colors, spacing, typography, and breakpoints, through a configuration file.

To begin, create a configuration file using the following command:

```
npx tailwindcss init
```

This command will generate a `tailwind.config.js` file in the root directory of your project. The initial configuration file will look something like this:

```js
module.exports = {
  purge: [],
  darkMode: false,
  theme: {
    extend: {},
  },
  variants: {},
  plugins: [],
}
```

Theme customization

To customize the Tailwind CSS theme, you can add your own options within
the `theme` object. For example, if you want to change the default colors,
you can do so in the following way:

```
module.exports = {
  // ...
  theme: {
    extend: {
      backgroundColor: {
        'primary': '#1D1D1D',
        'secondary': '#2A2A2A',
      },
      textColor: {
        'primary': '#FFFFFF',
        'secondary': '#CCCCCC',
      },
    },
  },
  // ...
}
```

In this example, we have added two new background colors and two new
text colors, which will now be available in the project as utility classes.

Breakpoint customization

To customize breakpoints, add your options within the `screens` object in
the theme:

```js
module.exports = {
  // ...
  theme: {
    screens: {
      'xs': '480px',
      'sm': '640px',
      'md': '768px',
      'lg': '1024px',
      'xl': '1280px',
    },
    // ...
  },
  // ...
}
```

In this example, we added an `xs` breakpoint and modified the default values for the other breakpoints.

Tailwind CSS utility classes (advanced)

Tailwind CSS utility classes are at the heart of the framework and allow you to create flexible and responsive user interfaces. Let's delve into some of the main categories of utility classes:

Spacing

Tailwind CSS provides a set of utility classes for managing space between elements, such as margins and padding. The spacing classes follow the syntax `{properties}{sides?}-{size}`.
For example:

- `mt-4`: Sets a margin-top of 4 units.
- `pb-8`: Sets a bottom padding (padding-bottom) of 8 units.

- `mx-auto`: Centers an element horizontally by setting the left and right margins (margin-left and margin-right) to `mx-auto`.
- `space-x-4`: Sets a horizontal space of 4 units between the child elements of a flex or grid container.

Typography

Tailwind CSS includes utility classes to manage typography, such as font size, font weight, letter spacing, and line height. For example:

- `text-lg`: Sets the text size to `large`.
- `font-bold`: Sets the font weight to `bold`.
- `tracking-wide`: Sets a wider letter spacing between letters.
- `leading-relaxed`: Sets a wider row height.

Layout

Tailwind CSS offers utility classes to control the layout of your elements, such as display, position and overflow. For example:

- `block`: Sets the element as `block`.
- `inline-block`: Sets the element as `inline-block`.
- `absolute`: Sets the position of the element as `absolute`.
- `relative`: Sets the position of the element as `relative`.
- `overflow-hidden`: Hides excess content within the element.

Flexbox and Grid

Tailwind CSS includes utility classes for working with Flexbox and Grid, facilitating the creation of complex, responsive layouts. For example:

- `flex`: Sets the element as a flex container.
- `flex-wrap`: Allows flex child elements to wrap.
- `grid`: Sets the element as a grid container.
- `grid-cols-3`: Divides the element into three columns.

Creating custom components in Tailwind CSS (advanced)

Tailwind CSS allows you to create custom components using predefined utility classes. This approach allows you to create reusable components that are consistent throughout your project. For example, imagine you want to create a "card" component:

```html
<div class="bg-white shadow-md rounded-lg p-4">
  <img class="w-full h-48 object-cover mb-4" src="path/to/image.jpg" alt="Image card">
  <h3 class="text-lg font-semibold">Title card</h3>
  <p class="text-gray-500">Card description</p>
</div>
```

In this example, we used Tailwind CSS utility classes to create a "card" component with an image, title, and description. Now you can reuse this component throughout your project.

Tailwind CSS extensions and plugins (advanced)

Although Tailwind CSS offers a wide range of utility classes and features, you may want to extend the framework with additional or custom functionality. This can be done through extensions or plugins.

Extensions allow you to add new utility classes to your project. To create an extension, add your custom classes inside the `extend` object in the configuration file:

```javascript
module.exports = {
  // ...
  theme: {
    extend: {
      // Your custom utility classes here
    },
  },
  // ...
}
```

Plugins, on the other hand, are external code packages that extend Tailwind CSS by adding new functionality or utility classes. To use a plugin, you must first install it as a dependency in your project and then add it to your configuration file.

For example, suppose we want to use the `tailwindcss-typography` plugin, which adds a number of utility classes for advanced typography. First, install the plugin using npm or yarn:

```
npm install @tailwindcss/typography
```

Or

```
yarn add @tailwindcss/typography
```

Next, add the plugin to your `tailwind.config.js` configuration file:

```js
module.exports = {
  // ...
  plugins: [
    Require('@tailwindcss/typography'),
    // More plugins here
  ],
}
```

Now, you can use the additional utility classes provided by the `tailwindcss-typography` plugin in your project.

In conclusion, Tailwind CSS is a flexible and customizable framework that allows you to create responsive user interfaces and designs with ease.

With its wide range of utility classes and the ability to create custom components and extend the framework with extensions and plugins, Tailwind CSS is a powerful and versatile tool for modern Web site development.

Insight

1. Introduction to CSS preprocessors:

Tailwind CSS can be used in conjunction with CSS pre-processors such as Sass, Less or Stylus. These tools offer advanced features such as variables, mixins, functions, and nesting, which can improve the productivity and maintainability of CSS code.

To integrate Tailwind CSS with a pre-processor, follow the specific documentation for your chosen pre-processor and configure your development environment to use both tools.

For example, to use Tailwind CSS with Sass, you can follow the instructions in the **official guide to Tailwind CSS for Sass** [(https://tailwindcss.com/docs/using-with-preprocessors)](https://tailwindcss.com/docs/using-with-preprocessors).

2. Performance optimization:

Performance optimization is critical to ensure that your website loads quickly and the user experience is smooth.

One of the techniques for optimizing performance with Tailwind CSS is to use PurgeCSS, which automatically removes unused CSS classes from your final CSS file.

To configure PurgeCSS, update the `purge` property in your `tailwind.config.js` file, indicating the file paths that contain the Tailwind classes:

```js
module.exports = {
  purge: ['./src/**/*.html', './src/**/*.js'],
  // ...
}
```

3. Examples of common layouts:

Tailwind CSS makes it easy to create common layouts such as sidebars,
card grids, and lists. For example, to create a grid of cards, you can use
the `grid` and `grid-cols-` utility classes:

```html
<div class="grid grid-cols-3 gap-4">
  <!- Cards here ->
</div>
```

To create a sidebar, use the `flex` or `grid` classes to create a two-column
structure, and then use the spacing classes to control the size and position
of the sidebar:

```html
<div class="flex">
  <aside class="w-64 p-4">Sidebar</aside>
  <main class="flex-1 p-4">Main content</main>
</div>
```

4. Animations and transitions:

Tailwind CSS offers utility classes for creating CSS animations and
transitions.
For example, to add a transition when the mouse hovers over an element,
you can use the `transition`, `duration-`, `ease-` and `transform` classes:

```html
<button class="bg-blue-500 hover:bg-blue-700 transition-colors
duration-300 ease-in-out">Click here</button>
```

5. Accessibility:

Accessibility is a crucial aspect of web design and development, as it ensures that your site is usable by people with disabilities.

Tailwind CSS includes utility classes to improve accessibility, such as `sr-only` (to hide content visually but make it accessible to screen readers) and `focus:outline-none` (to remove the default outline to the focus and add a custom style).

To ensure a high level of accessibility, follow WCAG guidelines and use tools such as **Lighthouse** [https://developers.google.com/web/tools/lighthouse) to check your site for compliance.

6. Integration with JavaScript frameworks:

Tailwind CSS can be easily integrated with popular JavaScript frameworks such as React, Vue, and Angular. To integrate it with React, for example, follow these steps:

- Install Tailwind CSS as a dependency of your project.

- Configure your development environment to use Tailwind CSS (see section 1 of the guide).

- Use Tailwind CSS utility classes in your React components.

An example of a React component with Tailwind CSS:

```jsx
import React from 'react';

function Button({ children, onClick }) {
  return (
    <button
     onClick={onClick}
     className="bg-blue-500 hover:bg-blue-700 text-white font-bold py-2 px-4 rounded"
    >
     {children}
    </button>
  );
}

export default Button;
```

7. Themes and skins:

Creating custom themes and skins with Tailwind CSS is easy because of its configurability.

You can edit the `tailwind.config.js` file to add new colors, change defaults, or extend existing classes.

For example, to add a new color theme, update the `theme` section in your configuration file:

```js
module.exports = {
  theme: {
    extend: {
      backgroundColor: {
        'theme-blue': '#1e90ff',
        'theme-green': '#32cd32',
      },
    },
  },
  variants: {},
  plugins: [],
};
```

Now you can use the new theme classes throughout your project, such as
`bg-theme-blue` and `bg-theme-green`.

8. Additional documentation and resources:

To learn more about Tailwind CSS, check out the **official documentation**
(https://tailwindcss.com/docs), which provides comprehensive guidance on
the framework's features and use.

Also, look for tutorials, videos and articles written by the developer
community to learn new tricks and techniques.

Join forums and discussion groups dedicated to Tailwind CSS to share your
experiences and learn from other developers.

Tailwind UI

Tailwind UI: a premium component library for Tailwind CSS.

Tailwind UI is a premium component library developed by the Tailwind CSS team, designed to simplify and speed up the development of responsive user interfaces and designs.

While Tailwind CSS is a utility-first framework that offers a set of atomic classes to create custom user interfaces, Tailwind UI builds on this approach by providing pre-built, ready-to-use components, all while maintaining the flexibility and aesthetics of Tailwind CSS.

Why use Tailwind UI?

1. Save time: Tailwind UI offers a wide range of pre-built components, such as tabs, modals, navigation bars, forms, tabs, and more. By using these components, developers can save time in creating user interfaces, focusing instead on the logic and functionality of the application.

2. Consistent Design: All Tailwind UI components are designed to be aesthetically consistent and follow Tailwind CSS design guidelines. This ensures that your website or application looks professional and consistent across all pages and sections.

3. Easy integration: Tailwind UI integrates seamlessly with Tailwind CSS and can be used in conjunction with the framework's utility classes and features. You can also extend and customize Tailwind UI components according to your specific needs.

4. Documentation and support: Tailwind UI comes with detailed documentation and code examples for each component, making it easy to implement and customize. In addition, the Tailwind CSS team offers direct support to Tailwind UI users, ensuring quick troubleshooting and question resolution.

How to use Tailwind UI with Tailwind CSS

To use Tailwind UI in your Tailwind CSS project, follow these steps:

1. Purchase a license: Tailwind UI is a commercial product and requires the purchase of a license to be used in your projects.
Visit the **Tailwind UI website** (https://tailwindui.com) to choose the license that best suits your needs.

2. Install the necessary dependencies: Make sure you have installed and configured Tailwind CSS in your project, as described in the basic guide.

Tailwind UI also requires the installation of some additional plugins, such as `@tailwindcss/forms`, `@tailwindcss/aspect-ratio`, `@tailwindcss/line-clamp` and `@tailwindcss/typography`.
Follow each plugin's documentation for installation and configuration.

3. Import Components: Once you have purchased the license, you will have access to Tailwind UI component files.
Import the components you wish to use in your project by copying the corresponding HTML code and pasting it into your HTML file or JavaScript component (if you are using a framework such as React, Vue, or Angular).

4. Customize components: Tailwind UI components are built using Tailwind CSS utility classes, which means you can easily customize them by adding, removing, or modifying utility classes found in the HTML code.

You can also use your Tailwind configuration file to customize colors, spacing, and other global CSS properties of components.

5. Adapt components to your needs: If necessary, you can combine and modify Tailwind UI components to create new elements or layouts that fit the specific needs of your project.

With the flexibility of Tailwind CSS's utility-first framework, you have the freedom to create unique, customized user interfaces without having to give up the consistency and ease of use of pre-built components.

In conclusion, Tailwind UI is an excellent resource for developers who wish to accelerate the development of responsive user interfaces and design using Tailwind CSS.

With its wide range of pre-built components, consistent design, and easy integration with Tailwind CSS, Tailwind UI allows you to quickly create high-quality websites and applications, saving time and resources in the process.

Here are 10 examples of components using Tailwind UI and Tailwind CSS.

Note that these examples are just snippets of HTML code and assume that you have already properly configured Tailwind CSS and Tailwind UI in your project.

1. Simple card

```html
<div class="bg-white p-6 rounded-lg shadow-lg">
  <h2 class="text-2xl font-semibold mb-2">Title Card</h2>
  <p class="text-gray-700">Description of the contents of the card.</p>
</div>
```

2. Navigation bar

```html
<header class="bg-gray-800 py-4">
  <nav class="container mx-auto flex items-center justify-between">
    <div class="text-white font-bold">Logo</div>
    <ul class="flex items-center space-x-4">
      <li><a href="#" class="text-white">Home</a></li>
      <li><a href="#" class="text-white">Products</a></li>
      <li><a href="#" class="text-white">Contacts</a></li>
    </ul>
  </nav>
</header>
```

3. Button

```html
<button class="bg-blue-600 text-white font-semibold px-6 py-2 rounded-md hover:bg-blue-500">Click me</button>
```

4. Contact form

```html
<form>
  <div class="mb-4">
    <label for="name" class="block text-gray-700 font-semibold">Name</label>
    <input type="text" id="name" class="w-full border-2 border-gray-300 p-2 rounded-md focus:border-blue-600">
  </div>
  <div class="mb-4">
    <label for="email" class="block text-gray-700 font-semibold">Email</label>
    <input type="email" id="email" class="w-full border-2 border-gray-300 p-2 rounded-md focus:border-blue-600">
  </div>
  <div class="mb-4">
    <label for="message" class="block text-gray-700 font-semibold">Message</label>
    <textarea id="message" rows="4" class="w-full border-2 border-gray-300 p-2 rounded-md focus:border-blue-600"></textarea>
  </div>
  <button type="submit" class="bg-blue-600 text-white font-semibold px-6 py-2 rounded-md hover:bg-blue-500">Submit</button>
</form>
```

<u>5. Product grid</u>

```html
<div class="grid grid-cols-3 gap-6">
  <div class="bg-white p-6 rounded-lg shadow-lg">
    <img src="https://via.placeholder.com/150" alt="Product" class="w-full h-48 object-cover mb-4">
    <h3 class="text-xl font-semibold mb-2">Product 1</h3>
    <p class="text-gray-700">$49.99</p>
  </div>
  <!-- Repeat product div for each grid element -->
</div>
```

<u>6. List with icons</u>

```html
<ul class="space-y-4">
  <li class="flex items--start">
    <i class="fas fa-check text-green-500 mr-2"></i>
    <p>Feature 1</p>
  </li>
  <li class="flex items-start">
    <i class="fas fa-check text-green-500 mr-2"></i>
    <p>Feature 2</p>
  </li>
  <li class="flex items-start">
    <i class="fas fa-check text-green-500 mr-2"></i>
    <p>Feature 3</p>
  </li>
  <!-- Add additional items to the list if needed -->
</ul>
```

7. Hero with call-to-action

```html
<section class="bg-blue-600 text-white py-16">
  <div class="container mx-auto text-center">
    <h1 class="text-4xl font-bold mb-6">Hero Title</h1>
    <p class="text-lg mb-6">Description of the hero section.</p>
    <button class="bg-white text-blue-600 font-semibold px-8 py-3
rounded-md hover:bg-gray-100">Find out more</button>
  </div>
</section>
```

8. Testimonials

```html
<div class="bg-gray-100 p--6 rounded-lg">
  <blockquote class="text-gray-700 italic mb-4">"The testimony of a
satisfied customer."</blockquote>
  <div class="flex items-center">
    <img src="https://via.placeholder.com/50" alt="Customer Name"
class="w-12 h-12 rounded-full mr-4">
    <div>
     <p class="font-semibold">Customer Name</p>
     <p class="text-gray-600">Role</p>
    </div>
  </div>
</div>
```

9. Pagination

```
<ul class="flex space-x-4">
  <li><a href="#" class="block px-4 py-2 border-2 border-blue-600 text-blue-600 rounded-md hover:bg-blue-600 hover:text-white">1</a></li>
  <li><a href="#" class="block px-4 py-2 border-2 border-gray-300 text-gray-700 rounded-md hover:border-blue-600 hover:bg-blue-600 hover:text-white">2</a></li>
  <li><a href="#" class="block px-4 py-2 border-2 border-gray-300 text-gray-700 rounded-md hover:border-blue-600 hover:bg-blue-600 hover:text-white">3</a></li>
</ul>
```

10. Footer

```
<footer class="bg-gray-800 py-8">
  <div class="container mx-auto grid grid-cols-4 gap-8 text-white">
    <div>
      <h3 class="text-xl font-semibold mb-4">Column 1</h3>
      <ul class="space-y-2">
        <li><a href="#" class="hover:underline">Link 1</a></li>
        <li><a href="#" class="hover:underline">Link 2</a></li>
        <li><a href="#" class="hover:underline">Link 3</a></li>
      </ul>
    </div>
    <!- Repeat column div for each column in the footer ->
  </div>
</footer>
```

These examples demonstrate how to use Tailwind UI and Tailwind CSS to create responsive and consistent design components.

You can further customize these components according to your needs and the specifications of your project.

Useful Resources

Below is a list of websites and resources that offer components and use cases for Tailwind CSS and Tailwind UI. These sites can help you find inspiration and resources for your projects.

1. **Tailwind UI (Official):** https://tailwindui.com
An official collection of high-quality, predefined components made by the Tailwind CSS team.

2. **Tailwind Components:** https://tailwindcomponents.com
A website with a collection of components created by the Tailwind CSS community, covering a wide range of design elements and use cases.

3. **Treact:** https://treact.owaiskhan.me
A collection of ready-to-use React components made with Tailwind CSS.

4. **Tail-Kit:** https://tail-kit.loafwallet.org
Tail-Kit offers over 350 free and premium components based on Tailwind CSS, covering a wide range of categories.

5. **Tailwind Toolbox:** https://www.tailwindtoolbox.com
Tailwind Toolbox offers a collection of free templates, components, and resources for Tailwind CSS.

6. **Meraki UI:** https://merakiui.com
Meraki UI is a collection of free design components and templates made with Tailwind CSS.

7. **Daisy UI:** https://daisy.js.org
Daisy UI is a plugin for Tailwind CSS that adds additional components and styles, making it easier to create consistent user interfaces and designs.

8. **Windy:** https://windy.vercel.app
Windy offers a collection of Tailwind CSS-based components that can be used in various projects.

9. **K-WD Dashboard:** https://k-wd-dashboard.web.app
A Tailwind CSS-based dashboard template that can be used as a starting
point for developing administration panels and dashboards.

10. **GitHub - aniftyco/awesome-tailwindcss:** https://github.com/
aniftyco/awesome-tailwindcss
A curated collection of Tailwind CSS related resources, components,
templates and tools available on GitHub.

These sites provide a variety of components and resources to help you
create responsive user interfaces and designs using Tailwind CSS and
Tailwind UI.

Explore them to find the inspiration and resources you need for your
projects.

Conclusion

In this ebook, we explored the potential of Tailwind CSS and Tailwind UI for creating responsive websites and design. We discussed the differences between Tailwind CSS and other frameworks, delved into the benefits of using Tailwind CSS, explained how to set up and use the framework, and provided numerous component examples and resources to help you get started.

We hope this information has been helpful and given you a solid foundation to start using Tailwind CSS in your projects. Remember, practice is key to mastering any new technology, so we encourage you to practice what you learned in this ebook and continue to explore the possibilities offered by Tailwind CSS and Tailwind UI.

Don't forget that learning is a journey and that every step counts. Don't be afraid to experiment and make mistakes along the way; it is these mistakes that will help you grow as a developer.

Turn your ambitions toward creating products and services that have a positive impact on people and the world. Work with passion, commitment and determination, and never stop improving. With Tailwind CSS and Tailwind UI as tools in your toolbox, you are on your way to achieving something great.

Keep on giving your best, learning and putting your knowledge into practice. With dedication, patience and a positive mindset, there is nothing you cannot accomplish. Good luck and happy programming!

"Success is not the key to happiness. Happiness is the key to success. If you love what you are doing, you will be successful."

Albert Schweitzer